WHO

IS

PRESIDENT

?

By Fannie T. Brown

ISBN: 978-1-4269-6596-8 (sc)
ISBN: 978-1-4269-6597-5 (e)

Trafford rev. 08/02/2011

 www.trafford.com

North America & international
toll-free: 1 888 232 4444 (USA & Canada)
phone: 250 383 6864 • fax: 812 355 4082

Acknowledgements

As I began to think of all the people to whom I would like to express my appreciation, I realized that the numbers are difficult to ascertain. So, with that in mind, first I would like to thank God for allowing me to bless others, and myself, through a fun-filled career as an educator, where I had an opportunity to see children mature into productive citizens. I would like to thank my mother who persuaded me to educate others and to write poems, not only to entertain, but also to educate. Also, I would like to thank my husband for his patience and support through the rearing of out two sons, and for his support of my hobby. I would like to thank my two sons for persuading to print the books so that others can enjoy the fun learning experiences, they enjoyed as children. I would also like to thank family, friends, supporters, and the states of North Carolina and South Carolina, for providing me support and the infrastructure to succeed.

Table of Contents

Introduction

Through history, the American presidents played an important role in national history. This book shows, through poetry and illustrations, some of the major events that took place during the administration of each American president.

He was called the "Father of Our Country."
He was our first president, you know.
He did not have an easy job,
helping this country to grow.
He was the greatest,
I'll tell you the reason why.
According to the legend,
he never told a lie

Name:	George Washington
Date of birth:	February 22, 1732
Place of birth:	Pope's Creek Plantation in Westmorland County, Virginia
Years in office:	1789-1797
Wife's name:	Martha Custis Washington
Children's Name:	Martha "Patsy" Parke Custis (step –child)

This man is really interesting!
He was president number two.
Because the country was so young,
He had a great deal of work to do.
He was the first president
to make the "White House" his home.
This house was so large to him,
he was almost never alone.

Name: John Adams
Date of birth: October 30, 1735
Place of birth: Braintree, Massachusetts
Years in office: 1797-1901
Wife's name: Abigail Adams
Children's Name: Abigail "Nabby" Adams Smith
                        John Quincy Adams
                        Susanna Adams
                        Charles Adams
                        Thomas Boylston Adams

His nickname was Mr. Mammoth,
and was president number three.
He was an inventor, a violinist,
and very talented you see!
While he was in office,
a polygraph was designed.
The function of this machine,
was to cut down writing time.

Name:	Thomas Jefferson
Date of birth:	April 13, 1743
Place of birth:	Shadwell in Goochland County, Virginia
Years in office:	1801-1809
Wife's name:	Martha Wayles Skelton Jefferson
Children's Name:	Martha Washington Jefferson Randolf
	Jane Randolf Jefferson
	Mary "Polly" "Maria" Jefferson Eppes
	Lucy Elizabeth I
	Lucy Elizabeth II

The War of 1812 was fought,
while he was serving as president.
Washington, D.C., also was burned,
and that's the way "it" went.

Name:	James Madison
Date of birth:	March 16, 1751
Place of birth:	Port Conway, Virginia
Years in office:	1809-1817
Wife's name:	Dolley Payne Todd Madison
Child's Name:	John Payne Todd

When this man was president,
He started a "public high school."
The Monroe Doctrine of 1823,
was also his favorite rule.

Name:	James Monroe
Date of birth:	April 28, 1758
Place of birth:	Westmoreland County, Virginia
Years in office:	1817-1825
Wife's name:	Elizabeth Monroe
Children's Name:	Elizabeth Kortright Monroe Hay
	J.S. Monroe
	Maria Hester Monroe Gouverneur

He was the son of our second president,
and our sixth president, you know.
He was president for only four years,
but most people love him so!

Name:	John Quincy Adams
Date of birth:	July 11, 1767
Place of birth:	Briantree, Massachusetts
Years in office:	1825-1829
Wife's name:	Louisa Catherine Adams
Children's Name:	George Washington Adams
	John Adams II
	Charles Frances Adams
	Louisa Catherine Adams

He was the seventh president,
"Old Hickory" was his nickname.
He was the best loved and most hated president,
this country has ever seen!

Name:	Andrew Jackson
Date of birth:	March 15, 1767
Place of birth:	Waxhaw, North Carolina
Years in office:	1829-1837
Wife's name:	Rachel Jackson
Child's Name:	Andrew Jackson, Jr.

This man was really a "trick,"
he was president number eight.
He was called the "Little Magician,"
because his accomplishments were so great.

Name:	Martin Van Buren
Date of birth:	December 5, 1782
Place of birth:	Kinderhook, New York
Years in office:	1837-1841
Wife's name:	Hannah Hoes Van Buren
Children's Name:	Abraham Van Buren
	John Van Buren
	Martin Van Buren, Jr.
	Smith Thompson Van Buren

This man was president number nine.
He had ten children,
and his wife was very kind.
He crushed the Shawnees,
at the battle of Tippecanoe.
His campaign was based on the slogan,
"Tippecanoe and Tyler, too."

Name:	William Henry Harrison
Date of birth:	February 9, 1773
Place of birth:	Charles City County, Virginia
Years in office:	1841 (died on his 32nd day in office)
Wife's name:	Anna Tuthill Symmes Harrison
Children's Name:	Elizabeth "Betsey" Bassett Harrison Short
	John Cleves Symmes Harrison
	Lucy Singleton Harrison Este
	William Henry Harrison, Jr.
	John Scott Harrison
	Benjamin Harrison
	Mary Symmes Harrison Thornton
	Carter Basset Harrison
	Anna Tuthill Harrison Taylor
	James Findlay Harrison

He was the tenth president of the United States.
He became president when Harrison died.
He knew a lot about politics,
and the "difficult things," he tried!
During the time he was president,
Florida became a state.
The telegraph between Washington and Baltimore,
was also very great.

Name: John Tyler
Date of birth: March 29, 1790
Place of birth: Charles City County, Virginia
Years in office: 1841-1845
Wife's name: Letitia Christian Tyler and
                       Julia Gardiner Tyler

Children's Name: Mary Tyler Jones
                       Robert Tyler
                       John Tyler, Jr.
                       Letitia (Letty) Tyler Semple
                       Elizabeth "Lizzie" Tyler Waller
                       Anne Cotesse Tyler
                       Alice Tyler Denison
                       Tazewell Tyler
                       David Gardiner "Gardie" Tyler
                       John Alexander "Alex" Tyler
                       Julia Tyler Spenser
                       Lachlan Tyler
                       Lyon Gardiner Tyler
                       Robert Fitzwalter Tyler
                       Pearl Tyler Ellis

He was our eleventh president,
and he served four long years.
Even though his job was hard,
he had very little fears.

Name:	James K. Polk
Date of birth:	November 2, 1795
Place of birth:	Mecklenburg County, North Carolina
Years in office:	1845-1849
Wife's name:	Sarah Childress Polk
Child's Name:	Marshall Polk (nephew and ward)

He was called "Old Rough and Ready,"
because he stood so tall.
He was our twelfth president,
and to our country, he gave his all.

Name:	Zachary Taylor
Date of birth:	November 24, 1784
Place of birth:	Orange County, Virginia
Years in office:	1849-1850
Wife's name:	Margaret Mackall Smith Taylor
Children's Name:	Anne Margaret Mackall Taylor Wood
	Sarah "Knox" Taylor Davis
	Octavia Pannel Taylor
	Margaret Smith Taylor
	Mary Elizabeth Taylor Bliss Dandridge
	Richard Taylor

Uncle Tom's cabin was published

He was born in the state of New York,
a very long time, ago.
He was our thirteenth president,
and his name, I am sure you will know.

Name: Millard Fillmore
Date of birth: January 7, 1800
Place of birth: Cayuga County, New York
Years in office: 1850-1853
Wife's name: Abigail Powers Fillmore
Children's Name: Millard Powers Fillmore
                         Mary Abigail "Abby" Fillmore

He was born in Hillsboro, New Hampshire,
as our fourteenth president.
His reputation as a great politician,
followed him where he went.
He served four years as president
and his wife's name was Jane.
His three children died at an early age,
and this incident caused great pain.

Name:	Franklin Pierce
Date of birth:	November 23, 1804
Place of birth:	Hillsboro, New Hampshire
Years in office:	1853-1857
Wife's name:	Jane M. Pierce
Children's Name:	Franklin Pierce
	Frank Robert Pierce
	Benjamin Pierce

He was our fifteenth president.
As a leader, he wasn't very great.
He tried to stop the Civil War,
but his help came too late!

Name:	James Buchanan
Date of birth:	April 23, 1791
Place of birth:	Cove Gap, Pennsylvania
Years in office:	1857-1861
Wife's name:	Harriet Lane-deceased fiancé
Children's Name:	None

He was our sixteenth president,
and was not very rich, but brave!
While he served as president,
he vowed to free the slaves.

Name: Abraham Lincoln
Date of birth: February 12, 1809
Place of birth: Hardin County, Kentucky
Years in office: 1861-1865
Wife's name: Mary Todd Lincoln
Children's Name: Robert Todd Lincoln
                           Edward Baker "Eddie" Lincoln
                           William Wallace "Willie" Lincoln
                           Thomas "Tad" Lincoln

When he was young, he was very poor.
He became a tailor and suffered no more.
After Lincoln died, he became president,
and he also ratified the thirteenth Amendment.

Name:	Andrew Johnson
Date of birth:	December 29, 1808
Place of birth:	Raleigh, North Carolina
Years in office:	1865-1869
Wife's name:	Eliza McCardle Johnson
Children's Name:	Martha Johnson Patterson
	Charles Johnson
	Mary Johnson Stover Brown
	Robert Johnson
	Andrew Johnson, Jr.

He was our eighteenth president,
and as a soldier, he was great!
During the time he was president,
Colorado became a state.

Name:	Ulysses S. Grant
Date of birth:	April 27, 1822
Place of birth:	Point Pleasant, Ohio
Years in office:	1869-1877
Wife's name:	Julia Dent Grant
Children's Name:	Fredrick Dent Grant
	Ulysses Simpson "Buck" Grant, Jr.
	Ellen Wrenshall "Nellie" Grant Sartoris Jones
	Jesse Root Grant

He was our nineteenth President,
a lawyer, a congressman, and a governor.
He also served in the Civil War!
Hard times brought on a nationwide strike,
and Thomas Edison invented a bulb of a light.

Name:	Rutherford B. Hayes
Date of birth:	October 4, 1822
Place of birth:	Delaware, Ohio
Years in office:	1877-1881
Wife's name:	Lucy Webb Hayes
Children's Name:	Birchard Austin Hayes
	James Webb Cook Hayes
	Rutherford Platt Hayes
	George Crook Hayes
	Fanny Hayes Smith
	Manning Force Hayes

He was the twentieth president,
and his term was very short.
However, he was able to start the "Red Cross."
Therefore, he never really lost!

Name:	James Abram Garfield
Date of birth:	November 19, 1831
Place of birth:	Moreland Hills, Ohio
Years in office:	1881
Wife's name:	Lucretia Rudolph Garfield
Children's Name:	Eliza Arabella "Trot" Garfield
	Harry Augustus "Hal" Garfield
	James Rudolf Garfield
	Mary "Mollie" Garfield Stanley-Brown
	Irvin McDowell Garfield
	Abram Garfield
	Edward Garfield

He was a lawyer and a senator,
and our twenty-first president, too!
When he became president,
he had a lot to do.

Name:	Chester Alan Arthur
Date of birth:	October 5, 1829
Place of birth:	Fairfield, Vermont
Years in office:	1881-1885
Wife's name:	Ellen Lewis Herndon Arthur
Children's Name:	William Lewis Arthur
	Ellen Herndon "Nell" Arthur Pinkerton

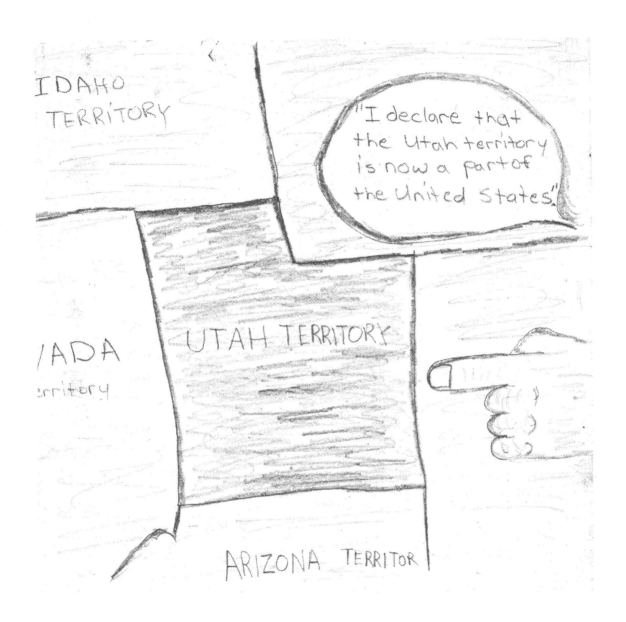

He was our twenty-second president,
and also president number twenty-four.
He helped Utah to become a state,
and he did a great deal more!

Name:	Grover Cleveland
Date of birth:	March 18, 1837
Place of birth:	Caldwell, New Jersey
Years in office:	1885-1889 and 1893-1897
Wife's name:	Frances Folsom Cleveland
Children's Name:	Oscar Folsom Cleveland
	Ruth Cleveland
	Esther Cleveland Bosanquet
	Marion Cleveland Dell Amen
	Richard Folsom "Dick" Cleveland
	Francis Grover Cleveland

His soldiers called him "Little Ben,"
when he and Sherman came marching in, (Atlanta)
Oklahoma was open to settlement,
after he became president.

Name: Benjamin Harrison
Date of birth: August 20, 1833
Place of birth: North Bend, Ohio
Years in office: 1889-1893
Wife's name: Caroline Lavinia Scott Harrison
Children's Name: Russell Benjamin Harrison
                         Mary "Mamie" Scott Harrison McKee
                         Elizabeth Harrison Walker

He was president number twenty-two and twenty-four.
The years he served were four and four.
He dedicated the "Statue of Liberty" in his first
administration.
At this time, the Henry Ford cars were all over the nation.

Name:	Grover Cleveland
Date of birth:	March 18, 1837
Place of birth:	Caldwell, New Jersey
Years in office:	1885-1889 and 1893-1897
Wife's name:	Frances Folsom Cleveland
Children's Name:	Oscar Folsom Cleveland
	Ruth Cleveland
	Esther Cleveland Bosanquet
	Marion Cleveland Dell Amen
	Richard Folsom "Dick" Cleveland
	Francis Grover Cleveland

This man was really someone!
He was president number twenty-five.
Gold was discovered in Alaska,
while he was still alive.

Name: William McKinley
Date of birth: January 29, 1843
Place of birth: Niles, Ohio
Years in office: 1897-1901
Wife's name: Ida Saxton McKinley
Children's Name: Katherine "Katie" McKinley
                         Ida McKinley

This man was our twenty-sixth president,
and he loved to hunt and ride.
He was president for eight long years,
and he had a great deal of pride!
While he served as president,
Oklahoma became a state.
He also started the FDA,
and that was something great!

Name:	Theodore Roosevelt
Date of birth:	October 27, 1858
Place of birth:	New York, New York
Years in office:	1901-1909
Wife's name:	Edith Kermit Carow Roosevelt
Children's Name:	Alice Lee Roosevelt Longworth
	Theodore "Ted" Roosevelt, Jr.
	Kermit Roosevelt
	Ethel Carow Roosevelt Derby
	Archibald "Archie" Bulloch Roosevelt
	Quentin Roosevelt

He was a lawyer and a judge,
and our twenty-seventh president, too.
He helped to start the "parcel post,"
which means a lot to you.

Name:	William Howard Taft
Date of birth:	September 15, 1857
Place of birth:	Cincinnati, Ohio
Years in office:	1909-1913
Wife's name:	Helen Herron Taft
Children's Name:	Robert Alphonso Taft
	Helen Herron Taft Manning
	Charles Phelps Taft

This man was a teacher,
and he became a lawyer, too!
As our twenty-eighth president,
he had a lot to do.
When he was president,
we had the beginning of World War I,
and the nineteenth Amendment
let women enjoy the work they had done.

Name:	Woodrow Wilson
Date of birth:	December 28, 1856
Place of birth:	Staunton, Virginia
Years in office:	1913-1921
Wife's name:	Ellen Louise Axson Wilson and Edith Bolling Galt Wilson
Children's Name:	Margaret Woodrow Wilson
	Jessie Woodrow Wilson Sayre
	Eleanor "Nellie" Randolph Wilson McAdoo

He was a newspaper publisher,
and a senator you know!
Born in the village Corsica,
which later became Blooming Grove, Ohio.
He was the United States President number twenty-nine.
The trying days after the Civil War,
gave him a very hard time.

Name:	Warren Gamaliel Harding
Date of birth:	November 2, 1865
Place of birth:	Corsica near Blooming Grove, Ohio
Years in office:	1921-1923
Wife's name:	Florence Kling Harding
Children's Name:	Eugene Marshall "Pete" DeWolfe
	Elizabeth Ann (Ann) Christian Blaesing

He was our thirtieth president,
and he didn't often smile.
The things he did with his life,
made our lives worthwhile.
When he served as president,
we made our first phone call overseas,
and also, the first flight around the world
to help satisfy our needs.

Name:	Calvin Coolidge
Date of birth:	July 4, 1872
Place of birth:	Plymouth, Vermont
Years in office:	1923-1929
Wife's name:	Grace Goodhue Coolidge
Children's Name:	John Coolidge
	Calvin Coolidge, Jr.

His name was very familiar,
he was president number thirty-one.
When he was in office,
the "Great Depression" had begun.

Name:	Herbert Clark Hoover
Date of birth:	August 10, 1874
Place of birth:	West Branch, Iowa
Years in office:	1929-1933
Wife's name:	Lou Henry Hoover
Children's Name:	Herbert Hoover, Jr.
	Allan Henry Hoover

He was our thirty-second president,
and he served for twelve long years.
Although he had a case of polio,
he never shed a tear.

Name: Franklin Delano Roosevelt
Date of birth: January 30, 1882
Place of birth: Hyde Park, New York
Years in office: 1933-1945
Wife's name: Eleanor Roosevelt
Children's Name: Anna   Eleanor   Roosevelt   Dall   Boettiger
Halsted

James "Jimmy" Roosevelt
Franklin Roosevelt
Elliot Roosevelt
Franklin Delano Roosevelt, Jr.
John Aspinwall Roosevelt

He was our thirty-third president,
and he served for eight long years.
He was elected near the end of World War II,
when the nation was filled with fear.

Name:	Harry S. Truman
Date of birth:	May 8, 1884
Place of birth:	Lamar, Missouri
Years in office:	1945-1953
Wife's name:	Elizabeth "Bess" Wallace Truman
Children's Name:	(Mary) Margaret Truman Daniel

He was our thirty-fourth president,
His nickname was "Ike."
He always kept a smiling face,
And he was a man that anyone could like.

Name:	Dwight David Eisenhower
Date of birth:	October 14, 1890
Place of birth:	Denison, Texas
Years in office:	1953-1961
Wife's name:	Mamie Doud Eisenhower
Children's Name:	Doud Dwight (Ikky) Eisenhower
	John Sheldon Doud Eisenhower

This was a very special president,
he was president number thirty-five.
If he had not been assassinated,
he would probably be alive.
He accomplished a lot in a very short time,
and he may have been one of the best in his time.

Name:	John Fitzgerald Kennedy
Date of birth:	May 29, 1917
Place of birth:	Brookline, Massachusetts
Years in office:	1961-1963
Wife's name:	Jacqueline Kennedy Onassis
Children's Name:	Caroline Kennedy Schllossberg
	John Fitzgerald Kennedy, Jr.
	Patrick Bouvier Kennedy

He became President, after Kennedy died,
And he won the 1964 election by a landslide.
The Vietnam conflict he tried to win,
but it made the American people think "it" was sin.

Name:	Lyndon Baines Johnson
Date of birth:	August 27, 1908
Place of birth:	Stonewall, Texas
Years in office:	1963-1969
Wife's name:	Claudia Johnson
Children's Name:	Lynda "Lady" Bird Robb
	Luci Baines Johnson Turpin

While this man was president,
we never got a break,
to really enjoy T.V.,
there was always "Watergate!"
He was our president, number thirty-seven,
and someone who was very slick,
but everyone knew that "Watergate,"
was something he could not fix.

Name:	Richard Milhous Nixon
Date of birth:	January 9, 1913
Place of birth:	Yorba Linda, California
Years in office:	1969-1974
Wife's name:	Patricia Nixon
Children's Name:	Tricia Nixon Cox
	Julie Nixon Eisenhower

This man was president number thirty-eight,
and he became president because of "Watergate."
There were so many challenges written on the wall,
it seemed as if he could never complete a thing at all.
He tried to revive a depressed economy,
and he tried to master inflation,
but everyone began to complain
as they went to the "gas-station."
He was also a man who tried to heal the land,
but it seemed as though things kept getting out of hand.

Name:	Gerald Rudolph Ford
Date of birth:	July 14, 1913
Place of birth:	Omaha, Nebraska
Years in office:	1974-1977
Wife's name:	Elizabeth "Betty" Ford
Children's Name:	Michael Gerald Ford
	John "Jack" Gardner Ford
	Steven Meigs Ford
	Susan Ford Vance Bales

He lived in Plains, Georgia.
He was president number thirty-nine.
It seems his fame came,
in the nick-of-time.
He tried to free the hostages from Iran,
but the helicopters crashed in the desert sand!
What a costly mistake for the president,
known as "The Peanut Man."

Name: Jimmy Earl (Jimmy) Carter
Date of birth: Plains, Georgia
Place of birth: October 1, 1924
Years in office: 1977-1981
Wife's name: Rosalynn Carter
Children's Name: John Williams "Jack" Carter
                       James Earl "Chip" Carter III
                       Donnell Jeffrey "Jeff" Carter
                       Amy Carter Wentzel

He was the fortieth President.
He served from 1981 to 1989.
When he took office,
the economy was fine.
He got the hostages from Iran,
but prices were rising as fast as they can.
He was shot by a would-be assassin,
and this caused a great big roar.
Because of this terrible incident,
his popularity began to soar.

Name:	Ronald Wilson Reagan
Date of birth:	February 6, 1911
Place of birth:	Tampico, Illinois
Years in office:	1981-1989
Wife's name:	Nancy Reagan
Children's Name:	Maureen Reagan Revell
	Michael Reagan
	Patricia "Patti Davis" Ann Reagan
	Ronald Prescott Regan

This man was elected president in 1988,

and his greatest test came, when the Iraqi military invaded

Kuwait.

When he took office he had done so many things,

he had been the youngest pilot in the Navy,

to receive his wings.

Fifty-eight combat missions he flew.

Remember, these combat missions

were flown during World War II.

Name:	George Herbert Walker Bush
Date of birth:	June 12, 1924
Place of birth:	Milton, Massachusetts
Years in office:	1989-1993
Wife's name:	Barbara Bush
Children's Name:	George Walker Bush
	Pauline Robinson "Robin" Bush
	John Ellis "Jeb" Bush
	Neil Mallon Bush
	Marvin Pierce Bush
	Dorothy "Doro" Bush Kock

"THE BUDGET IS BALANCED"!

He was the first "Baby-Boomer" president thus far,
and he was elected at the end of the Cold War.
He was known as the "Comeback Kid,"
and among the tallest presidents in history.
The things he achieved as president,
will always remain a mystery.
He was American president number forty-two.
Balancing the budget, he had to do,
to save this great country,
for you and me, too.

Name:	William Jefferson (Bill) Clinton
Date of birth:	August 19, 1946
Place of birth:	Hope, Arkansas
Years in office:	1993-2001
Wife's name:	Hillary Rodham Clinton
Child's Name:	Chelsea Victoria Clinton

When he was president, the World Trade Center came down.
Anyone that heard it will never forget the sound.
What an awful sight this was,
for all Americans to see.
Meanwhile, people from around the world watched on T. V.
So, he sent our troops to Iraq,
in search for W.M.D.
He did not find weapons of mass destruction,
as he searched this land.
He did find Saddam Hussein,
who he thought was a very evil man.

Name:	George Walker Bush
Date of birth:	July 6, 1946
Place of birth:	New Haven, Connecticut
Years in office:	2001-2008
Wife's name:	Laura Bush
Children's Name:	Barbara Pierce Bush
	Jenna Welch Bush

His battle for the Presidency was something the world had never seen.

Mainly because his middle name was the last name of Saddam Hussein.

To be selected his party's nominee, was something American's never expected to see,

because his party opponent, just happen to be a "she."

"She" was the wife of a former president, and everyone knew her name.

Running against this woman, was like adding fuel to the flame.

While an old grey-haired man for the Republican Party ran his election race behind a "Bush,"

no one expected that this would give, the president to be, a push.

He was American president number forty-four.

Oh! Let me tell you just a little bit more.

He was the first African-American President, he was elected president in 2008.

This sent a message to young Americans, that it's never too late, to set "your goals" now, and include the way you want the world to be.

Of course the legacy of this man, will be written by you and by me, as people from around the world, will be watching him on HD-TV.

Name:	Barrack Hussein Obama
Date of birth:	August 4, 1961
Place of birth:	Honolulu, Hawaii
Years in office:	2008-present
Wife's name:	Michelle Obama
Children's Name:	Malia Ann Obama
	Natasha "Sasha" Obama